NORTH AMERICAN INDIAN PORTRAITS

PHOTOGRAPHS FROM THE WANAMAKER EXPEDITIONS

NORTH AMERICAN INDIAN PORTRAITS

PHOTOGRAPHS FROM THE WANAMAKER EXPEDITIONS

FROM THE WANAMAKER COLLECTION
AT THE
WILLIAM HAMMOND MATHERS MUSEUM
INDIANA UNIVERSITY

INTRODUCED BY

THOMAS W. KAVANAGH

CURATOR OF COLLECTIONS
WILLIAM HAMMOND MATHERS MUSEUM

KONECKY & KONECKY

Konecky & Konecky
72 Ayers Point Road
Old Saybrook, CT 06475
www.koneckyandkonecky.com

10 digit ISBN: 1-56852-755-1
13 digit ISBN: 978-1-56852-755-0

Book design by STUDIO 31, INC.

Printed in India

Frontispiece: [w3602] White Hawk (Northern Cheyenne)

CONTENTS

(The reference numbers that appear throughout the text and accompany
the photographs correspond to the Mathers Museum Catalog.)

INTRODUCTION

The Wanamaker Collection at the William Hammond Mathers Museum, Indiana University, is a unique record of American Indians — and of the ways non-Indians viewed Indians — during the first decades of the twentieth century. Under the sponsorship of John and Rodman Wanamaker of Philadelphia, and directed by Joseph Kossuth Dixon, the three "Wanamaker Expeditions to the American Indian" of 1908, 1909, and 1913, produced more than 11,000 still photographs and several miles of movie film. In later years, Dixon documented Indian participation in World War I through both photographs of the veterans and through individual questionnaires; that project culminated in the participation of the Crow chief Plenty Coups in the dedication of the Tomb of the Unknown Soldier at Arlington National Cemetery in 1921.

Following the deaths of both Dixon and the Wanamakers — John Wanamaker in 1922, Dixon in 1926, and Rodman Wanamaker in 1928 — their Indian materials were dispersed. Many of the photographs, negatives and prints, along with other papers and documents came to Indiana University via the Arthur H. Jordan Foundation of Indianapolis, and directly from the Wanamaker store, in the 1940s. Other materials, including glass and nitrate negatives, were sent to the University Museum in Philadelphia, and the American Museum of Natural History in New York; the surviving movie film is at the National Archives in Washington, D.C. The American Museum donated their nitrate negatives to Indiana University in 1972.

Although most of the movie film and many of the still pictures, photographed on volatile nitrate-based celluloid film, disintegrated as early as the 1920s, the Wanamaker Collection at the Mathers Museum contains almost 37,000 original items, comprising almost 8,000 glass and nitrate film negatives, and almost 30,000 original photographic prints (including enlargements up to 22 by 29 inches) and photogravure reproductions; the Wanamaker Collection at the Mathers Museum also includes several thousand letters, notes, and other documents relating to the Expeditions, as well as the questionnaires received back from the World War I veterans. It is the largest collection of photographs of American Indians by a single photographic enterprise in the United States. In contrast, although it is said that Edward S. Curtis may have made more than 40,000 photographs in a comparable time span, only about 2,200 Indian images were ever published, and none of his original negatives survive.

Despite its massive size, very little of the purposes of the Wanamaker Expeditions and the extent of the resulting photographic and documentary collections is generally known. In large part, this was due to the way its creators brought the photographs to the attention of the public: only about

350 images, less than four percent of the estimated 11,000 original negatives — less than five percent of the surviving negatives — were ever published during lifetimes of either Dixon or the Wanamakers. In turn, that has resulted in the reputation of the Dixon-Wanamaker photographs as a romanticizing of Indian life.

While it is true that the published images were probably selected for their image qualities, the photographs in the Wanamaker Collection are not all of one piece, and the images presented here are only a small selection of the whole. We have included sensitive and technically superb individual portraits, documentary photographs of contemporary conditions, quick but often flawed snapshots, and staged representations of the popular stereotype of The Indian as splendidly mounted and feathered Plains warriors, exemplar of a romantic but tragically doomed Vanishing Race.

In offering this selection, we have included a number of images which have been have been previously published, but the majority have not. We have included selections from each of the three major Expeditions, although we have emphasized the portraits from 1913. We have included both individual portraits — thus our title — as well as other documentary photographs. For some of the images, a good deal of contextual information — biographical, ethnographic, and historical — is available or can be deduced from other sources; indeed, we have been able to contact some of the living descendants of the represented individuals and have thus been able to link both the continuing family and the museum collection. Wherever possible, we have provided a glimpse of that available information. Moreover, we continue to add to our documentation, and further identifications are appreciated.

A VANISHING RACE?
THE WANAMAKER EXPEDITIONS TO THE AMERICAN INDIAN

John Wanamaker was an American original. Born in 1837 — or 1838, the records are unclear — in Philadelphia, the son of a brick maker, he grew up to become a multimillionaire, "the greatest merchant in America." He established the first department store — although he never used the term — invented the money-back guarantee, and was called the father of modern advertising, the prince of advertisers. But in many ways he was also a hold over from an earlier time in American business; at a time when cutthroat business practices were common, Wanamaker maintained a concern for the welfare of both his customers and his employees. Both his Philadelphia and New York stores had large auditoriums in which he sponsored concerts — the Wanamaker Organ (formerly installed at the 1898 St. Louis Exposition) is still one of the world's largest pipe organs — and lectures on uplifting subjects.

Many of the concerts were directly sponsored by Rodman Wanamaker, second son of the founder. Born in 1863, Rodman served as manager of the Paris store 1888–1898, of the New York store from 1911, and full owner of the chain from 1920. Rodman was far more outgoing than either his older brother, Thomas B. — owner and editor of the *Philadelphia North American* newspaper — or his father. He had a large art collection, a major collection of stringed instruments (including four Stradivarius violins, and one Stradivarius viola). He was also an enthusiastic supporter of powered flight, supporting both airplane designer Glenn Curtiss and the explorer Richard E. Byrd.

In 1906, John Wanamaker hired Joseph Kossuth Dixon to be director of the Education Bureau in his stores, responsible for arranging the lectures, in many cases giving the lectures himself, and a publication program, including a series of primers — short books — for young people. Dixon was born in 1856 in Hemlock Lake, New York, the son of British immigrants; the family later moved to Leavenworth, Kansas. Dixon attended a small college in Missouri, and later the Rochester Theological Seminary, receiving a Bachelor of Divinity degree. Although he later called himself Doctor, the doctorate was apparently self-bestowed. Dixon held pastorates in New York state, Providence, Rhode Island, and in Philadelphia; it was at these labors that Dixon perfected a style of expression full of grandiloquence and bombast, but regrettably often short on substance. By 1904 Dixon was working for the Eastman Kodak photographic company, giving lectures on such topics as "The Kodak: a Moral Force," and in 1906 he went to work for the Wanamakers.

By 1908, Dixon had began to focus his attention on American Indians. While it is clear that the Wanamaker family had a longstanding interest in Indians — in the 1850s, John Wanamaker had visited an Indian community in Indiana; in the 1880s, students from nearby Carlisle Indian School worked at the Wanamaker store; and in the early twentieth century Wanamaker had sponsored several collecting expeditions for the University Museum of the University of Pennsylvania — and Dixon often claimed a lengthy study of Indians, the extent of his own knowledge is uncertain.

One idea was fundamental to Joseph Dixon and the Wanamakers in their Indian projects: race. However, to call them racist would be to call up the modern negative connotations of that term, many of which did not exist at the turn of the century; racialist may be a better term. In the early years of the twentieth century, race was a constant in everyday discussions. But it was often an uninvestigated constant. Everyone knew that races existed, but there was a looseness in how people discussed them. People spoke of the American race, the Jewish race, the African race, and so on, as singularities, each with typical behavioral characteristics.

With the concept of race, whole populations could be lumped

together and summarized in a few key images, in stereotypes. While some of the specifics of Indian stereotypes changed over time, by the twentieth century a multi-faceted composite image of Indians had emerged. Dixon's particular version, as stated in his Primer, was that the Indian — note the singular — by virtue of being Indian, was "dignified and graceful," . . . "a warrior," . . . "an orator," and so on. But despite these virile qualities, it was inevitable that the Indian race would soon vanish before the march of Anglo-Saxon civilization. As Dixon stated in *The Vanishing Race*,

> all serious students of Indian life and lore are deeply convinced of the insistent fact that the Indian, as a race, is fast losing its typical characters and is soon destined to pass completely away.

The idea of Indians as a "vanishing race" had its origins in the eighteenth century; perhaps its greatest expression was in James Fenimore Cooper's *The Last of the Mohicans* and Henry Wadsworth Longfellow's *The Song of Hiawatha*. Indeed, it was the latter which inspired Dixon's first Indian project. In the summer of 1908, directly sponsored by Rodman Wanamaker, and with a small staff that included his son Rollin, Dixon traveled to the Crow Indian Reservation in Montana to dramatize and film *The Song of Hiawatha* using the Crow Indians as its actors. That project neatly characterizes the summary nature of the Indian stereotype, for the original poem was an admixture of Algonquian mythology with Iroquois names — one observer noted, "If a Chinese traveller, during the middle ages, inquiring into the history and religion of the western nations, had confounded King Alfred with King Arthur, and both with Odin, he would not have made a more preposterous confusion of names and characters." Dixon's filming of it along the Little Bighorn [W1015] only added another level of conflated imagery. Unfortunately, the movie film disintegrated in the 1920s; but some 1400 glass and nitrate images relating to the making of the movie and to other scenes in and around Crow Agency survive in the Wanamaker Collection.

Still following the image of a "vanishing race," in 1909 Dixon gathered about fifty chiefs — actually relatively few were political leaders — from several Plains and Plateau tribes at the Crow Reservation to participate in what he called the "Last Great Indian Council." Dixon interviewed the men about their life histories, especially their war exploits, and staged a sham battle. Afterwards, they rode off symbolically into the sunset. A number of those interviews, together with portraits and other photographs, were published in Dixon's *The Vanishing Race* (1913). Some 1500 other images survive in the Wanamaker Collection.

That same year, 1909, Dixon and the Wanamakers undertook their largest project: a massive National Indian Memorial to be built on Fort

[W339] Eli Blackhawk as Hiawatha, Angela Star Blackhawk as Minehaha and Wolf Lies Down as the Arrowmaker

Wadsworth island in New York harbor; the statue would be larger than the Statue of Liberty. Then, in 1913 after the ground-breaking ceremony for the Memorial, concluding that one solution to Indian poverty would be the granting of American citizenship to Indians, Rodman Wanamaker sponsored the "Expedition of Indian Citizenship." Again with a small staff in a special railroad car equipped with a photographic studio, Dixon traveled to over 250 reservations and Indian communities asking individuals to sign a "Declaration of Allegiance" and to pledge loyalty to the American Flag. Along the way he made portraits of many of the signers of the Declaration.

At the outbreak of World War I, Dixon testified before Congress that the Army should take advantage of the Indian's innate abilities and form separate all-Indian cavalry scout regiments. Although the Army did not take up that racially based proposal, they did make use of Indian cultural abilities: an all-Choctaw telephone squad was established using the Choctaw language as an unbreakable code. After the War, Dixon photographed both the veterans — including the telephone squad — and the battlefields on which they fought in preparation for a book *From Tepees to Trenches*. Perhaps because his primary photographer had been wounded in the War — suggesting that Dixon himself made the images — the three hundred photographs of the veterans are the least technically proficient of the entire collection.

11

By the twentieth century, much of the Indian cultures had changed, often in the face of forced assimilation and acculturation by the dominant forces of the Euroamerican societies. In the first decades of the twentieth century, many anthropologists were involved in what was called "salvage ethnography," the hurried recording of the last vestiges of traditional culture.

In *The Vanishing Race*, Dixon suggested one potential value of his photographs:

> So rapidly are the western tribes putting aside their native customs and costumes, their modes of life and ceremonies, that we belong to the last generation that will be granted the supreme privilege of studying the Indian in anything like his native state . . . All future students and historians, all ethnological researches must turn to the pictures now made and the pages now written [i.e. *The Vanishing Race*] for the study of a great race.

But here is a multiple irony. On the one hand, in the very decades that Dixon worked, the self-described Indian population of the United

[W2556] Plenty Coups (Crow) greeting Two Moons (Northern Cheyenne) at the Last Great Indian Council, 1909

[W3170] Cut Finger (Southern Arapaho) signing the Declaration of Allegiance at El Reno, OK, June 21, 1913.

States slowed its decline, and the Bureau of Indian Affairs declared that the number of Indians was rising. Dixon, of course, would have none of it. Once again confusing race and culture, he declared those new figures to be a statistical fraud: they included mixed-bloods and even whites who lived with the Indians. At the same time, although the anthropologists collected masses of traditional information, they did very little participant observation on contemporary Indian cultures. That is, although there were more anthropologists in the field, they were recording very little of what they actually saw, and thus the Indian cultures of around the turn of the century are very little known. But that is exactly where the Wanamaker photographs are most valuable. While the prose in *The Vanishing Race* is of little continuing ethnological value in the study of Indians — although of value as reflections of how non-Indians viewed Indians — the photographs — although taken as representations of a timeless native state — are in fact

13

[w6367] Corporal Roy LaValle (Cree), United States Marine Corps, on board the battleship U.S.S. Utah, in New York harbor, April 29, 1919.

representations of the Indian cultures in the first decades of the twentieth century. In that context, they can have great historical and ethnographic value.

READING PHOTOGRAPHS

There is a style of photographic interpretation, with some ties to the old beliefs of phrenology — the study of the bumps on the head — which holds that one can read character in the face. Dixon himself was not above that style: his title for the full length portrait of Wolf Lies Down (w827) is Grand Old Face.

A more objective style of ethnographic interpretation is called "reading photographs." It endeavors to identify as many of the elements in a photograph as possible, from the identity of the subject to all of the artifacts visible; it passes beyond the individual image to the entire body of images made by the photographer, and the entire body of photographs of the social group in question. Sometimes those dimensions lead to dead ends, sometimes they reveal entire cultural and social dimensions hidden in the image.

A photograph is a selective recording of a visual scene. The camera does not see all, and what it sees can be intentionally manipulated both by the photographer and by the subject.

[w3617] Standing Bear

[w3623] Powder Face

Understanding the degree of photographic manipulation is necessary for the evaluation of any particular image or set of images. One of the most common ways photographers manipulated Indian images was through the use of studio props. In much the same way that "old-time" photographers today have a stock of clothing in which to "dress up" their customers, early photographers often had a stock of "Indian" objects — clothing, headdresses, subjects. Thus, one of the first steps in evaluating a set of photographs is to look for objects which appear in more than one photograph. Significantly, there is very little evidence of such manipulation in Dixon's photographs.

One of the few examples is a pair of photographs from the 1913 expedition showing two men from the Fort Belknap Reservation in Montana, one an Assiniboine, the other a Gros Ventres, wearing the same beaded leather shirt, headdress and gun case. Although Standing Bear wears the shirt in the photographs of the signing of the Allegiance at Fort Belknap — suggesting that they were indeed his clothes — it is not known who — Dixon or the men themselves — decided to have the two men wear the same clothes.

15

[W2671A; W2671B; W1485A] Sunset of a Dying Race

A more common manipulation represented in the Wanamaker Collection is the use of darkroom techniques to manipulate the atmosphere — the background, sky, or clouds — of a photograph. There are several examples in the Wanamaker Collection which show such photographic manipulation to enhance the image. The most obvious is "The Sunset of a Dying Race."

This image began in 1909, when Dixon had the participants in his Last Council ride over a hilltop while he photographed them. From one of the negatives of this series, he then prepared an overlay of celluloid to block out two of the figures. For the final print, the sky was artificially darkened to simulate a sunset.

Still another form of image manipulation is the stereotype, using a single image to stand for the whole. For instance, the image of Indians presented through the published photographs was one in which most evidence

[W1759] Mountain Chief

[W2126] Dr. Dixon welcoming Blackfeet [Mountain Chief on the right]

of Euro-American artifacts was removed, and the subjects are wearing their best "Indian clothes."

In the accompanying photograph Mountain Chief is dressed in the classic Blackfeet "straight up" headdress; it and his shirt are literally dripping with white ermine tails; there is a stuffed animal at his left shoulder. He holds a wooden horse effigy — said by his family to represent a favorite horse, one he stole from the Crows, and which once, although severely wounded, came back to his lodge.

This image might leave the impression that Indians wore those traditional clothes into the twentieth century. However, the Wanamaker Collection also includes snapshots showing more informal and daily dress.

In the second photograph, Mountain Chief — on the right — wears a three piece western-cut suit, a watch fob, and a broad brimmed hat. Indeed, all of the Indians in this photograph wear Euroamerican clothes; the only visible clue to their Indian identity is their braided hair, and the one feather; indeed, there is no reason to suspect that these are not their normal "good clothes." Ironically, it is Dixon who is dressed up in a costume — crowned campaign hat, riding britches, leather leggings, and high boots.

In this regard, it may be noted that although there is romanticism in the photographs in the Wanamaker Collection, it is as much the result of how the Indians presented themselves as how Dixon represented them.

DIXON AND CURTIS

As a photographer of and writer about American Indians in the early twentieth century, Dixon's work invites inevitable comparison to that of Edward S. Curtis. Indeed, such comparisons began even as the work was in progress: in 1913, James McLaughlin, former Agent at the Standing Rock reservation, and now Inspector for the Indian Service detailed to accompany the Citizenship Expedition, offered this evaluation of the enterprise:

> It is true that Dr. Dixon has visited every tribe of importance in the United States. As to the records made by him, that is another question. Although not an artist, it seems to me that the pictures made by the Expedition are very fine indeed — as pictures. But as records, either of the Indian as he was or of the Indian as he is, they are of no value whatever. . . . There is no comparison between these hastily-snapped pictures, and those which represent the lifework of artists from Catlin to Deming, and of photographers such as Haynes, Barry, and Curtis.

There are indeed many obvious contrasts with Curtis, both in the photographs and the accompanying written materials. For instance, Curtis

[W3254] Canyon de Chelly

was in the midst of a massive project: a forty-volume compendium of information. Twenty volumes would be text with some photographs, while the other twenty volumes would be photographs alone. Dixon, too, professed to "gather historic data [on Indians]and make picture records of their manners, customs, their sports and games, their warfare, religion, and the country in which they live." But despite his pretensions, Joseph Dixon was no scholar; indeed one searches his papers in vain for references to any original research beyond the 1909 interviews with the chiefs. Moreover, many of the "facts" as published in *The Vanishing Race* are either incorrect or misconstrued. Although *The Vanishing Race* continues to be in print, and is often quoted by researchers — particularly the interviews relating to the Battle of the Little Bighorn — its text must be used with extreme caution; as one member of the Citizenship expedition wrote (confidentially) to McLaughlin, Dixon's report contained "misinformation, . . . weird, impractical ideas, and even downright falsehoods." Dixon was hostile to criticism; in 1912, John W. Sanborn — who had been writing and lecturing on the Seneca since at least 1878 — wrote to him correcting several errors in the Primer: that the Iroquois were not, strictly speaking, an Atlantic coast people, and that the use of the word "tribe" to refer to the Iroquois as a whole was a misnomer; both were valid if minor criticisms. Dixon scrawled the word "Bosh" across the letter.

On the other hand, there are obvious photographic parallels between Dixon and Curtis. For instance Dixon's photograph of Navajo riders in the Canyon de Chelly is very similar to Curtis's images of the canyon. But before we too readily agree with Curtis that Dixon's photographs were "fakey imitations" of his own work, we should also note that as makers of images, both Dixon and Curtis shared a common vision of The Indian. Moreover, that vision was shared by many other photographers. Both Curtis and Dixon [w3261] photographed Navajo women seated at their looms; so did Ben Wittick and James Mooney in the 1880s and 1890s. Dixon's view of the 1908 Crow Fair encampment on the Little Big Horn [w392] is remarkably similar to both Curtis's view "On the Little Bighorn," and to views made by Fred Miller, an employee of Crow Agency. As with Curtis's 1907 view of Walpi village on First Mesa, Dixon's 1913 view [w3292] is so close as to suggest that there were markers in the ground saying, "place your tripod here." But to say that one or the other originated the image while the other merely copied it would be to place too much emphasis upon the originator and not enough on the images.

Nonetheless, the Dixon photographs, and the Wanamaker Collection as a whole, have several qualities which set them apart from Curtis. Not the least of these is that many, if not most, of the images are presented as portraits of real people. That is, while there are the inevitable titled images — "Watching the Dance," "Down a Western Slope," or "The Attack" — for the most part the subjects of the photographs are presented not as stereotypes but as identified and identifiable individuals. From that comes the realization that some of these individuals were alive in our own lifetimes.

PHOTOGRAPHS
FROM THE
WANAMAKER
EXPEDITIONS

CUSTER SCOUTS ON THE BATTLEFIELD
(CROW)

WO523

In 1876, a number of Crow Indians enlisted as scouts — "wolves" — for the U.S. Army, serving against their enemies, the Lakota Sioux. Six went with Lt. Col. George A. Custer and the 7th Cavalry: Half-Yellow Face, White Swan, White Man Runs Him, Hairy Moccasin, Goes Ahead, and Curly. At the Little Bighorn, while Half-Yellow Face and White Swan went with Major Marcus Reno, the others went with Custer. Before charging the village, Custer told the scouts with him they could leave. They stayed around for a short time, then went north to the Yellowstone where they found Gen. Alfred Terry, and told him of the battle.

In later years, the battle site was within the Crow Reservation and the Crow scouts frequently recounted their exploits for visitors. Dixon made portraits of the scouts both in 1908 and in 1909.

WHITE MAN RUNS HIM
(CROW)

W0240

One of the Custer Scouts. Dixon was very fond of White Man Runs Him and had first suggested that he be invited to lay the wreath on the Tomb of the Unknown Soldier. At the last minute, Plenty Coups went instead.

PLENTY COUPS
AN IMPERIAL WARRIOR:
A MOUNTED CHIEF
(CROW)

W0761

Plenty Coups — his name is better translated as Many Accomplishments — carried the pipe as leader of the Crow scouts who went with Three Stars, General George Crook, in the campaigns of 1876.

In the early 1880s, he and his band of about 20 families established ranches along Pryor Creek on the western part of the Crow Reservation where he built a two-story log and frame house. On one of his later trips to Washington, D.C. on tribal business, he visited Mount Vernon and the Tomb of George Washington. While there, he got the idea to donate his house and property to the tribe as a park; it is now a Montana state park.

An account of his early life was written by Frank Linderman; of his later life, Plenty Coups refused to speak.

OLD COYOTE
(CROW)

WO173

Old Coyote was one of the scouts with Crook at the Battle of the Rosebud, June 16, 1876.

A VANISHING RACE
[GRAY BULL]
(CROW)

WO775

One afternoon in 1908, Dixon took Gray Bull to make a series of photographs. Towards dusk, Dixon positioned Gray Bull for a symbolic ride into the sunset. The image became emblematic of Dixon's view of Indians as a "Vanishing Race."

WOLF LIES DOWN
(CROW)

WO827

According to Gray Bull, a warrior who captured a gun from an enemy was entitled to trim his shirt with ermine skins.

Although Wolf Lies Down was long married, he had no children.

INDIAN VILLAGE

W0392

TIPI STUDY

W0910

INDIAN VILLAGE

W1015

These views are of the same encampment, taken on the banks of the Little Big Horn near the town of Crow Agency; the occasion was the annual Crow Fair.

The birchbark canoe, totally out of place on the Little Bighorn, was used in the farewell scenes of the Hiawatha movie. It was the second canoe used; the first was destroyed in a prairie fire which burned the barn in which it was stored.

This was a popular scene for photographers; Edward Curtis photographed it, as did Fred Miller, an amateur photographer who lived on the Crow Reservation.

BUFFALO: THE REST HOUR

W1041

TIN-TIN MEET-SA
(CAYUSE UMATILLA)

w1636

Tintin Meetsa's father, who held the same name, signed the June 9, 1855 Treaty with Governor Isaac Stevens. He was later head chief of the Cayuse, and owned over 4,000 horses. In 1909, the son was more than 80 years old and blind.

English speakers have long been in the habit of writing Indian words as hyphenated syllables. Unfortunately this tendency avoids approaching Indian words as real words. Dixon's hyphenation has been preserved in the titles of the photographs.

DR. DIXON INTERVIEWING
THE UMATILLA CHIEFS
[UMAPINE AND TINTIN MEETSA]

W1642

The Umatilla interpreter, Leo Sampson, sits at the far left while Rollin K. Dixon on the right takes notes. It was in interviws like this that Dr. Dixon obtained the stories of the chiefs for his book *The Vanishing Race*.

UMAPINE
(CAYUSE UMATILLA)

w1646

Umapine was born in 1845. In the Bannock and Paiute War of 1878, Umapine lured the Paiute war leader Egan into a trap; Egan and twelve others were killed, five were taken prisoner and over 300 horses were captured. Umapine died December 23, 1924 at age 79. However, one vainly searches the splendid portrait of Umapine for some clue of General Oliver Otis Howard's assessment of him as a "cruel and wicked man."

TANEHADDLE
(KIOWA)

W1650

Tanehaddle, Running Bird, was also known as Pauahty, Bison Bull Approaching. Born in 1846, Tanehaddle was active in the Southern Plains wars of the 1860s and early 1870s. He was also a Buffalo Doctor, dealing in bleeding wounds such as gunshot and arrow wounds. As a doctor, he remained active through the 1920s, attending to returning veterans of World War I.

KOON-KAH-ZAH-CHY
APACHE JOHN
(NAISHAN DENE)

wi658

The Naishan Dene, Plains or Kiowa Apaches, are distant relatives of the Apaches of the southwest. A small tribe, they allied themselves with the Kiowas, thus the name "Kiowa Apache." In *The Vanishing Race,* Dixon lumped them with the southwestern Apaches.

The Apache census for 1901 translates Koonkahzahchy as Defending His Camp. In the 1890s, Apache John had been a judge on the Court of Indian Offenses on the Kiowa Comanche Apache Reservation. He was also an important Roadman in the Native American Church and often spoke against state and national legislation that would ban the religious use of Peyote.

JACK RED CLOUD
(OGLALA LAKOTA)

WI668

Jack Red Cloud was the son of Red Cloud, the *Ite Sica* Bad Face Oglala leader. In his story of the Custer fight as given in *The Vanishing Race,* he implies that he was present at the battle, but other sources suggest that he was not. In 1890-91, he took an active, if sometimes hostile role, in the events following the massacre at Wounded Knee Creek.

TIPI OF BLACKFOOT

W1776

Although clearly arranged for the photgraph, this image shows some of the accoutrements brought to the Last Council by the Blackfoot delegation. The spear second from the left shows Mountain Chief's horse effigy (see W1759 in the introduction) while hanging from a lodgepole is a gun effigy. The grass around the fire pit has been carefully scraped away, and the bed areas have been edged with logs and packed with grass padding.

TWO MOONS
(NORTHERN CHEYENNE)

W1780

Two Moons was born in 1842, son of an Arikara man and a Cheyenne woman. In 1876, Two Moons was chief of a small band of Northern Cheyennes fighting at the Little Big Horn. After their surrender in 1877, he and a number of his Cheyennes served as scouts for General Nelson Miles. He was later considered by some to be "head chief" of the Northern Cheyennes.

CHIEF TWO MOONS
AS HE FOUGHT CUSTER

WI804

MARY BEAR TUSK
(NORTHERN CHEYENNE)

W1851

Mary Bear Tusk wears a trade cloth — a type of heavy woolen cloth, usually made in red or blue, and with a wide white selvedge edge — dress decorated with dentalia shells and metal sequins. Around her neck she wears a hair pipe bone and glass bead necklace.

Dentalia are long mollusk shells traded from the Pacific coast. "Hair pipes" are bone — formerly clam shell — beads commercially made in New Jersey for the Indian trade.

BESSIE STANDING ELK
AND THERESA SCALP CANE
(NORTHERN CHEYENNE)

w1865

Bessie Standing Elk and Theresa Scalp Cane wear trade cloth dresses decorated with dentalium, metal sequins, and ribbon work along the lower hem. Both also wear the german-silver (nickle silver) concho belt with a long side trailer favored by women on the northern Plains.

PLENTY COUPS
(CROW)

W1872

CURLEY
(CROW)

W1901

One of Custer's scouts (See w0523).

GOES AHEAD
(CROW)

WI895

Another of Custer's scouts (see WO523).

PRETTY SHIELD
[MRS GOES AHEAD]
PINNING TIPI (CROW)

W2061

Pretty Shield was a member of the Sore Lip Clan of the Mountain Crow. Her father was Kills in the Night, her mother was Crazy Sister in Law. Her uncle — mother's brother — was Half Yellow Face, leader of the Custer scouts.

Pretty Shield was a medicine woman in her own right. A biography by Frank Linderman, mostly in her own words, was originally published as *Red Woman,* recently reissued as *Pretty Shield.*

Goes Ahead died in 1919, and in 1924, both Pretty Shield's son, Good Goes Ahead, and daughter, Helen (see W1908), died leaving six children for Pretty Shield to care for. She filed a Widows Certificate with the War Department for her husband's pension, but by 1925, with no word on it, she appealed to Joseph Dixon for assistance. At his instigation, a Special Investigator was appointed but it is not known if the pension was granted.

HELEN GOES AHEAD
(CROW)

w1908

Daughter of Goes Ahead and Pretty Shield, Helen Goes Ahead married George Hogan, employee of the Crow Agency, with whom she had six children. Helen died in 1924.

TAKES-FIVE
(CROW)

W2013

Takes Five played "Old Nokomis" in the 1908 production of Hiawatha.

EVA SUN GOES SLOW
(CROW)

W2021

Eva Sun Goes Slow played some of the role of "Minehaha" in Hiawatha. In this photograph she is wearing the Minehaha dress.

THE NOON-DAY MEAL:
STRIKES FIRST AND WOLF PLUME
(BLACKFOOT)

W2112

Wolf Plume had served several terms on the Blackfoot Tribal Council when this picture was taken.

Wolf Plume and Strikes First had ten children, but all died in infancy.

MOUNTAIN CHIEF IN THE DANCE
(PIEGAN BLACKFOOT)

W2164

As a young man, Mountain Chief had gone on war expeditions against the Crows and sang of them. In the early 1900s, he served serveral terms on the Blackfoot Tribal Council.

In W1759 in the introduction, Mountain Chief holds a wooden horse effigy representing a favorite war horse.

As with many details in *The Vanishing Race,* Dixon got some things right, but confused others. Dixon called Mountain Chief the "hereditary chief of the Fast Buffalo Horse band." However, Fast Buffalo Horse was the personal name of the chief of the Blood band of Piegans.

FORDING THE LITTLE BIGHORN

W2188

As part of the Last Great Council activities, the chiefs went for an extended ride along the Little Bighorn River while Dixon and his crew photographed them. Although dramatic, the clouds in this photograph are actually the result of darkroom manipulation.

A few of the chiefs can be recognized from their shirts, headdresses, or other accoutrements. Jack Red Cloud is at the end, Timbo and Tanehaddle are about half way up.

CHEROKEE NATION SIGNING
THE DECLARATION OF ALLEGIANCE;
TAHLEQUAH, OKLAHOMA

W3100

At each of the more than 200 stops of the Citizenship Expedition made during the summer and fall of 1913, Dixon performed a ceremony in which he played a gramaphone recording of a speech by President Woodrow Wilson, gave a speech himself, prayed over an American flag, had the Indians present jointly raise another flag (the many-stranded halyard can be seen in the background), gave each of the tribes present a flag, and had the Indians sign the parchment Declaration of Allegiance. Some of the Indians were then invited to give speeches, but Dixon was usually in a hurry to get to the next stop and so often cut them off.

Among the staff of the Citizenship expedition was a stenographer; he made a transcript of every speech and every reply. The original is in the National Archives in Washington; a copy, together with other papers relating to the Expedition, is in the James McLaughlin papers at the Assumption Abbey Archives, Richardton, North Dakota.

COL. ROBERT B. ROSS
(CHEROKEE)

W3104

Robert Bruce Ross was a grandson of Chief John Ross, who had unsuccessfully fought the removal of the Cherokees from Georgia after gold was discovered on their lands.

GROUP OF SEMINOLE
WOMEN AND CHILDREN

W3119

In 1842 at the end of the Seminole War, which had lasted for eight years, most of the tribe was forced to resettle in Oklahoma, where this photograph was taken.

HE-SEE-MOIE
(OSAGE)

w3136

Heska Molah, 'Walking Horn' or White Horn Walks, was of the Hoenekasheka clan. He died in 1914.

While raising the flag at Pawhuska, the rope broke. During the ensuing delay, many Osages left, and by the time the halyard was repaired, only about a dozen remained. McLaughlin commented: "It cannot be said that the Osage Indians are enthusiastic over an honor which brings them no benefits of a material sort."

SHON-KA-MOIE AND DAUGHTER
(OSAGE)

W3137

Shunka Molah 'Walking Dog' was Priest of the Gentle Sky Clan, and Chief of the Governor Joe Band of the Osages. He earned his first war honors in 1863, and in the early 1900s was one of only three living Osages who had earned all 13 honors.

RA-RUH-WAH-KUH
JOHN LOUWALK
(CHAUI PAWNEE)

W3157

Raruhwaáku, His Mountain, also called John Louwalk, was chief of the Chaui band of Pawnees. Although he spoke little English, he worked closely with a number of anthropological fieldworkers, providing song texts and other information.

For the Pawnees, blue is the symbolic color of the heavens, and the stars are the source of spiritual power. Thus when Dixon presented his American flag ceremony, the Pawnees interpreted it according to their own traditions. As stated by James Murie *(Sakúru' Taa* Coming Sun), Pawnee interpreter and author of several anthropological works on the Pawnee, in reply to Dixon:

> These Pawnees know the stars, and they understand the heavens, and they understand their importance . . . when they [first saw the American flag in 1819] they saw the blue, representing the blue skies ofthe heavens, and they saw the stars upon the blue, which they knew were from the heavens, they thought God must have put it into the hearts of the people to make such a flag, and they have honored it from that day to this.

94

PAWNEE COUNCIL AND DANCE HOUSE

W3161

When the Pawnees moved from Nebraska to Oklahoma in 1874, they built a few mud lodges — anthropologists and historians call them earth lodges — including this one used by the South Bands as a council house. Another mud lodge served as the Skiri band council house. Both were replaced by frame round houses in the 1920s, and were themselves replaced by a single round house for the entire tribe in 1980.

INTERIOR OF PAWNEE MUD HOUSE

W3162

TA-BA-THA-TE
CHIEF CUT FINGER
(SOUTHERN ARAPAHO)

W3174

Cut Finger (see also W3170 in the introduction) together with Hail, Black Man and Watanga'a Black Coyote, were prominent religious leaders. For Dixon's flag ceremony at El Reno, Cut Finger wore his painted shirt associated with his sacred society.

TAWAKONI JIM
(TAWAKONI WICHITA)

W3179

The Tawakonis were a small Caddoan-speaking tribe on the southern Plains related to the Wichitas, Wacos, Taovayas, and Kitsais. By the twentieth century, they had all consolidated into a single political tribe called the Wichitas. Tawakoni Jim was the last Principal Chief of the Wichitas.

SHO-WE-TIT|
BILLY THOMAS
(CADDO)

W3183

GERONIMO APACHE VILLAGE (CHIRICAHUA APACHE)

W3200

In early 1913, the remnants of the Chiricahua Apaches under Geronimo, who had been held as prisoners of war since their surrender in 1886 — since 1894 at Fort Sill — were offered the choice of staying at Fort Sill or moving to the Mescalero Reservation in New Mexico; 187 went to New Mexico while 84 stayed in Oklahoma. This photograph, taken June 25, 1913, must have been soon after their arrival in New Mexico.

HOSKA-YILITH-NA-GA
(NAVAJO)

W3232

Ashkii Yil Nagai, Young Man Who Walks With Him.

PESH-LA-KAI ATCIDI
(NAVAJO)

W3240

Peshlikai Atsidi Silversmith, a noted singer, was born about 1850. He was one of the first Navajo silversmiths; indeed, he later claimed that he and another were the first Navajo silversmiths to make solder, thus enabling the setting of turquoise in silver.

In the winter of 1898, Peshlikai Atsidi and his "outfit" of 16 families were given permission to graze their sheep on the west side of the Little Colorado, outside the reservation. The sheriff of Coconino County, later a state senator, attempted to collect a cash tax on each animal, forcing the Navajos back across the frozen river. In the crossing, they lost all their lambs, and many ewes.

A DAUGHTER OF THE DESERT
WITH ANNIE DODGE
(NAVAJO)

W3249

Henry Chee Dodge was a noted Navajo entrepreneur, tribal chief, and later first chairman of the Tribal Council. His younger daughter, Annie, was to be come nationally noted for her work in the tribal health department. In 1963 she was awarded a U.S. Presidential Medal of Freedom by President John F. Kennedy.

WOMAN WEAVING RUG
(NAVAJO)

W3261

Photographs of Navajo women at their looms have been a staple of photographers since the 1880s.

THE HOPI CORN GRINDER
(HOPI)

W3284

Grinding corn was, and still is, a daily task for Hopi women. The three mealing bins are of different coarseness.

The woman's wrapped hair signifies that she is married. She wears the traditional Hopi woman's black wool dress with a woven belt.

A HOPI POTTERY MAKER
WORKING WITH CLAY
(HOPI)

W3276

In contrast to the Hopi corn-grinder in W3284, this potter wears a European-style cotton blouse and skirt, but with a traditional woven belt and mocassins.

Although an ancient craft, by the early twentieth century, Hopi pottery-making was practiced mainly on First Mesa, mostly at Hano, the Tewa-speaking village on the other (north) end of the mesa from Walpi (W3292). The broad shoulders of the jar drying to the potter's right proclaims it to be in the so-called Sikyatki Revival style developed by the Hano potter Nampeyo.

VILLAGE OF WALPI
FROM THE LEFT
(HOPI)

W3292

The village of Walpi sits on the tip of First Mesa, 600 feet above the desert floor. The village was established after the Pueblo Revolt of 1680, when the villages moved to the mesa tops from the desert floor. Just below the edge of the mesa are the remains of sheep pens while corn fields can be seen out in the dry bed of Polacca Wash. On a clear day, one can see the San Franscisco Peaks, 100 miles away.

HAVASUPAI
BASKET MAKER

W3305

SAN CARLOS APACHE SUMMER TIPI
(SAN CARLOS APACHE)

W3316

A canvas tent has been pitched under a brush covered ramada. Hanging from the pole is a pitch-covered water basket. In the background is another brush covered ramada, this time with a canvas thrown over it.

LUISEÑO SWEATBATH

w3388

Semi-subterranean sweat baths were important aspects of Luiseño purification and curing rituals.

AMOS LITTLE
(HUPA)

W3405

Amos Little, about 13 years old, dressed for the dance in honor of Dr. Dixon, holds a traditional painted bow and a quiver of arrows. The large disks on the quiver are pearl buttons.

ISHI
(YAHI)

W3418

Ishi was the last survivor of the Yahi band of the Yana Indians of California. For some 20 years, after his family was massacred by whites, he lived alone in the rugged hills of Deer Creek. In 1911, hungry and exhausted, he made his way to Oroville, California. He was befriended by the staff of the University of California (at the time in San Francisco) Museum of Anthropology. He lived the last five years of his life at the Museum.

CHIEF TOM CHOCKTOOT
(PAIUTE, KLAMATH RESERVATION, OREGON)

W3424

Chief Tom Chocktoot was a headman of the Paiutes of the Klamath Reservation in Oregon. He was also a *puhagami,* a shaman. In 1897, he was jailed for a week for disobeying a government order prohibiting native curing practices.

MRS. SUSAN PAPALIUT
(WARM SPRINGS)

W3464

A MEDICINE MAN
STANDING NEAR A TIPI|
(UMATILLA)

W3478

This man was, unfortunately, not named. The use of ermine tails and the way he holds the wolf skin may be compared to that of Umapine (W1642) suggesting that this is a cultural form rather than a posing by Dixon. In his right hand he holds a copy of the National Indian Memorial magazine which was distributed at every stop along Dixon's tour.

HE-YUME-WAH-PAH-LILPT
JENNIE LAWRAY
(NEZ PERCE)

W3491

CHIEF REGIS
(COEUR D'ALENE)

W3508

In May 1867, as "captain" of the Soldiers of the Sacred Heart, a lay Jesuit order, the resident Jesuit priest ordered Regis and fifteen of the Soldiers to go to another reservation to arrest an Indian living with another man's wife. Regis resisted, but the priest insisted. Upon arrival, they found the other man surrounded by heavily armed men. Regis decided that since May was the sacred month of Mary, it would not be proper for the soldiers of Mary to desecrate it with warfare. Therefore they returned empty handed.

Regis was later one of the principal chiefs of the Coeur d'Alene, several times traveling to Washington D.C. on tribal business.

BLACKFOOT CAMP
AT TWO MEDICINE LAKE,
GLACIER NATIONAL PARK

W 3540

Arriving at the Blackfoot Reservation in Browning, Montana, the Citizenship Expedition spent several days making photographs at a "camp" in Glacier National Park, adjacent to the Reservation. In contrast to the tipi village at Crow Fair (W392), all of the activities and clothing were authentic; however, this picturesque encampment was for the benefit of photographers. Indeed, many other photographers made similar photographs in and around Glacier Park.

A BLACKFOOT TRAVOIS

W4034

The travois was a transport device used by the Plains Indians consisting of two poles joined together by a frame.

WOLF PLUME
(BLACKFOOT)

W3518

Wolf Plume had been among the Blackfoot delegation to Dixon's 1909 Last Council. He owned a Medicine Pipe, probably not this one, for Dixon photographed other Blackfoot men holding it. The pin hanging from his looped necklace is entitled "Judge" but the specifics are not known.

WHITE BIRD
(FLATHEAD)

W3572

After visiting the Blackfoot reservation, the Citizenship Expedition retraced its steps to the west, to attend the "First National Indian Congress" held in conjunction with the Spokane Fair, September 13–21, 1913. Little more is known about this "Congress" or its participants, many of whom Dixon posed in front of this tipi.

ALEX AND MAGGIE JOHNSON
(NESPELEM)

W3574

MRS. SADIE BOYD
AND CHILD
(NESPELEM)

W3577

The cradle boards of many tribes were similar in design, constructed to protect the baby's head. (See also W3759 and W3824)

DOG RUMP
(ASSINIBOINE)

W3614

The Assiniboines speak one of the four dialects of Sioux (the others are Santee-Sisseton, Teton, and Yankton-Yanktonai), calling themselves Nak'óta. Although it has long been suggested that the Assiniboines are an offshoot of the Yanktonais, the linguistic evidence shows equal distance between the dialects.

BLACK DOG
(ASSINIBOINE)

w3620

HAWK FEATHER
(ASSINIBOINE)

W3621

SITTING BEAR
(ARIKARA)

W3647

Sitting Bear was the leading Arikara chief around the turn of the twentieth century.

RED TOMAHAWK
(YANKTONAI)

W3661

In 1890, Red Tomahawk was Second Sergeant of the Standing Rock Reservation police. On December 15, 1890 he was with the detachment of police sent by then agent James McLaughlin to arrest the Hunkpapa leader Sitting Bull, considered by McLaughlin to be leader of the "hostile" element at Standing Rock. In the melee which followed, Red Tomahawk fired one of the fatal shots at Sitting Bull.

LUKE BLUE COAT
AND EAGLE CHASING GIRL
(MINICONJOU LAKOTA)

W3676

There are seven divisions of the Lakota or Teton Sioux, residing on reservations in North and South Dakota, Montana, and in Canada. Most Miniconjous live on the Cheyenne River Reservation in South Dakota. Most Brule are on the Rosebud Reservation — some are at the Lower Brule near the Missouri River — and most Oglalas are at Pine Ridge.

LAURA OWNS THE FIRE
(LOWER BRULE LAKOTA)

W3696

TASONKE WYAMMIYOMMI
WHIRLWIND HORSE
(OGLALA LAKOTA)

W3717

HERA KA WAKITA
LOOKING ELK
(OGLALA LAKOTA)

W3719

SARAH CRISPIN
(NORTHERN ARAPAHOE)

W3739

Sarah Crispin was the wife of Thomas Crispin, a member of the Northern Arapahoe tribal council.

MARY AGNES CRISPIN
(NORTHERN ARAPAHOE)

W3740

Daughter of Sarah and Thomas Cripsin.

TETON BILL
(BANNOCK)

W3750

Weedzwe, or Teton Bill, wears a rawhide and fur-wrapped sun shade.

BIRD RED AND
BABY IN UTE CRADLE
(SOUTHERN UTE)

W3759

JOHN DALE
(SOUTHERN UTE)

W3760

Although floral patterned beaded bandolier bags are usually associated with the Great Lakes region (see W3822) they were seen in
photographs of Utes, although the mechanism of trade is
unknown.

PE DAH NOH QUOD
(CHIPPEWA)

w3822

According to the documentation, this photograph was made at the Long Lake Reservation, Minnesota. However, Long Lake is one of the small Chippewa reserves in Ontario, Canada.

Pedahnohquod wears classic Chippewa floral-beaded leggings, apron or breechcloth, and vest, and topped off with two magnificent bandolier bags.

INDIAN MOTHER AND CHILD
(CHIPPEWA)

W3824

CLIFF DWELLING:
MESA VERDE NATIONAL PARK

W4045

On their way to Ignacio, Colorado, headquarters of the Southern Ute tribe, the Citizenship Expedition stopped off at the recently opened Mesa Verde National Park. As have many tourists since, Dixon set up his cameras on the overlook across from Cliff Palace.

PLAINS INDIAN MAN
MOUNTED ON HORSE

W 4092

This and the following photograph — both clearly posed — are examples of Dixon's romantic view of Indians.

PLAINS INDIAN MAN

W4095